ABOUT THE
ONE EARTH BOOKS

During its nearly one hundred years of educating the public about environmental issues, the National Audubon Society has rarely achieved anything as important as reaching out to the world's young people, the voices of tomorrow. For Audubon and its 600,000 members, nothing is so crucial as ensuring that those voices speak in the future on behalf of wildlife.

Audubon reaches out to people in many ways—through its nationwide system of wildlife sanctuaries, through research vital to helping set the nation's environmental policy, through lobbying for sound conservation laws, through television documentaries and fact-based dramatic films, through *Audubon* magazine and computer software, and through ecology workshops for adults and Audubon Adventures clubs in school classrooms. Each of these is critical to reaching a large audience. And now, with the Audubon One Earth books, the environmental community can speak to the youngest minds in our citizenry.

Audubon is proud to publish One Earth in cooperation with Bantam Books. In addition to bringing new information and experiences to young readers, these books will instill in them a fundamental concern for the environment and its decline at the hands of humanity. They will also, it is hoped, stimulate an undying interest in the natural world that will empower young people, as they mature, to protect the world's natural wonders for themselves and for future generations.

We at Audubon hope you will enjoy the One Earth books and that you will find in them an inspiration for joining our earth-saving mission. Young people are the hope for our future.

Christopher N. Palmer
Executive Editor
President, National Audubon
Society Productions

ONE EARTH

WHERE ARE MY SWANS, WHOOPING CRANES, AND SINGING LOONS?

RON HIRSCHI

Photographs by ERWIN and PEGGY BAUER and others

National
Audubon
Society

BANTAM BOOKS · NEW YORK · TORONTO · LONDON · SYDNEY · AUCKLAND

With thanks to Beverly

If you would like to receive more
information about the National Audubon Society write to:

National Audubon Society, Membership Department
950 Third Avenue, New York, NY 10022

WHERE ARE MY SWANS, WHOOPING CRANES, AND SINGING LOONS?
A Bantam Book / October 1992

Executive Editor: Christopher N. Palmer

Library of Congress Cataloguing-in-Publication Data
Hirschi, Ron.
        Where are my swans, whooping cranes, and singing loons? / by Ron Hirschi ; photographs by Erwin and Peggy Bauer.
        p. cm—(One earth)
    "A National Audubon Society book."
    Summary: Describes the lifestyle and habitat of the swan, whooping crane, and loon; how the destruction of wetlands threatens
their survival; and what we can do to save the animals.
    ISBN 0-553-07801-1.—ISBN 0-553-35470-1
    1. Wetland fauna—Juvenile literature. 2. Wetland fauna—United States—Juvenile literature. 3. Trumpeter swan—Juvenile
literature. 4. Whooping crane—Juvenile literature. 5. Loons—Juvenile literature. 6. Endangered species—United States—Juvenile
literature. [1. Swans. 2. Whooping crane. 3. Loons. 4. Rare animals. 5. Wildlife conservation.] I. Bauer, Erwin A., ill. II. Bauer,
Peggy, ill. III. Title. IV. Series: Hirschi, Ron. One earth.
QL113.8.H57   1992
333.95'8—dc20   91-13407   CIP   AC

Published simultaneously in the United States and Canada

Bantam Books are published by Bantam Books, a division of Bantam Doubleday Dell Publishing Group, Inc. Its trademark,
consisting of the words "Bantam Books" and the portrayal of a rooster, is Registered in U.S. Patent and Trademark Office and in
other countries. Marca Registrada. Bantam Books, 666 Fifth Avenue, New York, New York 10103.

PRINTED IN THE UNITED STATES OF AMERICA

0 9 8 7 6 5 4 3 2 1

INTRODUCTION

Wetlands come in many shapes, sizes, and types. They form at the edge of streams, rivers, lakes, and ponds as marsh, swamp, bog, or wet meadow. They are also found at the edge of the sea and in the middle of deserts, where the life-giving flow of water creates the miracle of an oasis.

Sadly, too many wetlands have been destroyed. Along with them, the delicate balance of nature has been threatened. Our ability to save wetland plants and animals reflects our ability to continue living on our planet. Join us now as we travel from the places where many of us live in comfort to wetlands where swans, whooping cranes, and loons need our help to save their vanishing homes.

Come walk with me past the houses crowding the lakeshore. Search all the edges that lead to where water lilies grow.

Then follow a frog from its marshy home.

Plop! It hops into the lake with a splash!

Blackbirds sing from their cattail home, where you might fish for a while for sunfish or bass.

Mallards and geese might nest in the marsh along the shore.

Muskrats and beavers might also build a home here in the lake.

But where are my swans? Where are the whooping cranes and the songs of the loons? Who let them vanish from sight and from sound?

Once they had more homes in marshes, rivers, and lakes. Then people came with guns, bulldozers, and dams. Wet places were drained.

Marshes were covered with highways, farms, and cities. Lakes and rivers were polluted or dried from too much use.

If more lakeshores were quiet, if water were clean and clear, if plenty of fish could be caught, then loons might appear year after year.

Loons would build their nests on small floating islands or along protected shores. They would hatch their babies and give them rides on their backs, if only we would save their homes.

But where
are the
swans . . .

and the
majestic,
dancing cranes?
Have they all
vanished with
wetlands
now gone?

Whooping cranes have always traveled far each season to find homes in wetlands where the weather is mild.

But now they must search harder than ever before to find sparkling waters.

They spend their winters in only one southern marsh. They feed as they wade in the warm Texas water . . .

and as soon as winter is over, they fly
far to the north.

Their journey is two thousand miles
long and their wings soon grow weary.
They must stop to rest.

Looking down in flight, the elegant cranes search a patchwork of farms and cities for a place to spend the night. Balanced on the wind, they drop from the sky at a bend in a river— where cottonwoods line a quiet backwater marsh. Here in this tiny wilderness, the cranes eat, then sleep.

Since crane resting marshes have disappeared, they must search even longer as they fly to the vast, safe wilderness of Canada's Wood Buffalo Park. Here in this nesting and summer home, whooping cranes try to survive.

Whooping cranes are in great danger. So few of them remain that we must save and restore wetlands, we must protect their summer and winter homes. Then they might slowly increase in numbers.

But what about swans?
Where can they rest and
where can they nest?

Trumpeter swans once were so common that they flew through all of our skies until people shot them for food, feathery down, and sport.

Now too much of their water is taken away for farming, and the swans are in great danger on their wintering grounds.

You can listen for the music of these wild swans when they fly over wide rivers and clean, quiet lakes. Won't you save their beautiful song?

Plenty of water and a safe place to nest will help them survive. Only you can help save enough wetlands for eating and swimming, for bathing, and for sleeping in peace.

AFTERWORD

For young readers, parents, teachers,
big brothers, and big sisters:

The lands bordering streams, rivers, lakes, ponds, and even the sea are often wet places known as marsh, swamp, bogs, wet meadow—or more broadly called wetlands.

Because these wetlands form where land and water meet, they ooze with life of all kinds. Plants and animals found on dry ground, as well as those that usually live a completely aquatic life-style, can be found there. But there are also many plants and animals unique to wetlands. Because of our continual destruction of these areas, many of the plants and animals most dependent on them are now on lists of threatened and endangered species. Swans, whooping cranes, and loons are only examples of wildlife we can help when we protect wetlands.

In recent decades, scientists have discovered that many types of frogs and salamanders are rapidly disappearing. The disappearance of these frogs, salamanders, and other wildlife shows us that the world is becoming unlivable for many creatures. Soon it may be unlivable for us, too. Perhaps because frogs and salamanders have always been so approachable and fun for kids to find and study, they can help us find ways to protect American wetlands and to solve larger environmental problems. Help your children follow frogs into the wetland world near you. Learn more about the needs of these small amphibians. Maybe they will show us how to save the world.

ACTIVITIES

Things you can do to help save swans, whooping cranes, loons, and other wildlife that need wetland homes:

- As a school project, adopt a local wetland or marshy lakeshore. Visit your wetland often, recording plants and animals you see. Through your school or local newspaper, tell others about what you discover.

- As a school project, create a small wetland on your school grounds. Others are restoring wetlands and will help you with your project. Check your library to locate these other wetland restoration efforts.

- Loons need you to help preserve lakes where they once nested. To learn how and where to build a loon nesting platform, write the North

American Loon Fund, RR 4, Box 240C, Meredith, New Hampshire 03253.

- Learn the calls of swans, whooping cranes, and loons by listening to tapes and records. You might also get to know the other wonderful sounds of wetland birds and other animals by listening carefully on your next visit to a marsh or lakeshore.

- Create a painting or poster for your local grocery store, showing other people the beauty and music of wetland wildlife. Wouldn't it be fun to play a tape recording of wetland wildlife in public places?

- Frogs and salamanders are disappearing. You can help by starting a frog savers' club. If you know where a frog pond is located, get to know it better. Keep it clean. Also draw pictures of the types of frogs you see and maps of the places where you see them. As you restore the pond and more frogs and salamanders return, update those pictures and maps.

About the Author

Ron Hirschi is a renowned environmentalist who worked as a habitat biologist before turning full time to writing and working with children. He now visits children in classrooms and communities nationwide, inspiring their curiosity and helping them to see that there are many things they can do in their own backyards to make our earth a better place.

Ron has written twenty books for children, including the acclaimed *Winter* and *Spring* books and the recently published Discover My World series.

About the Photographers

Erwin and Peggy Bauer and the other contributors are among the world's most highly regarded wildlife photographers. Together the Bauers have published over twenty-five books and countless articles about their worldwide photographic expeditions.

The swans featured in this book were photographed in Yellowstone National Park (Wyoming), along the Snake River in Grand Teton National Park (Wyoming), and in Red Rock Lake National Wildlife Refuge (Montana).

Whooping cranes were photographed on Matagorda Island and in Aransas National Wildlife Refuge (Texas).

Loons were photographed in the lakes of Wisconsin and Northwest Territory, Canada.